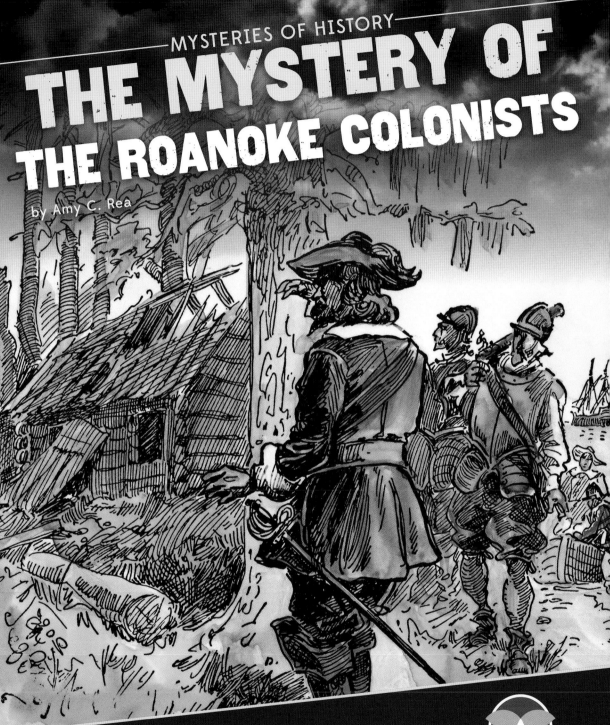

MYSTERIES OF HISTORY

THE MYSTERY OF
THE ROANOKE COLONISTS

by Amy C. Rea

Content Consultant
Eric Klingelhofer, PhD
Archaeologist
First Colony Foundation

Core Library

An Imprint of Abdo Publishing
abdopublishing.com

abdopublishing.com

Published by Abdo Publishing, a division of ABDO, PO Box 398166, Minneapolis, Minnesota 55439. Copyright © 2016 by Abdo Consulting Group, Inc. International copyrights reserved in all countries. No part of this book may be reproduced in any form without written permission from the publisher. Core Library™ is a trademark and logo of Abdo Publishing.

Printed in the United States of America, North Mankato, Minnesota
072015
012016

THIS BOOK CONTAINS
RECYCLED MATERIALS

Cover Photo: North Wind Picture Archives/AP Images
Interior Photos: North Wind Picture Archives/AP Images, 1; Public Domain, 4; Red Line Editorial/ Uxbona/NASA/JPL/NIMA, 7; US National Archives and Records Administration, 9, 43; Henry Howe, 12; John White, 14, 30, 34, 45; North Wind Picture Archives, 17, 19; William Segar, 22; English School, 16th century, 25; GraphicaArtis/Corbis, 28; Red Line Editorial, 32; Library of Congress, 37; AP Images, 39

Editor: Mirella Miller
Series Designer: Ryan Gale

Library of Congress Control Number: 2015945993

Cataloging-in-Publication Data
Rea, Amy C.
 The mystery of the Roanoke colonists / Amy C. Rea.
  p. cm. -- (Mysteries of history)
 ISBN 978-1-68078-026-0 (lib. bdg.)
 Includes bibliographical references and index.
 1. Roanoke Colony--Juvenile literature. 2. Roanoke Island (N.C.)--History--16th century--Juvenile literature.   I. Title.
 975.6--dc23
                                                                                2015945993

CONTENTS

CHAPTER ONE

LEAVING ENGLAND

England faced many problems in 1584. The country was crowded with people, and it was fighting an undeclared war on Spain. The two countries followed different religions, which caused tension. Spain had many advantages because of the wealth from its colonies in the West Indies, a chain of islands in the Caribbean Sea and the Atlantic Ocean. Spain had also started settling colonies in mainland

Queen Elizabeth of England wanted to earn more wealth for her country by establishing colonies.

Privateering: The Work of Pirates

Privateering was a way for countries to attack other countries' ships without declaring war. "Privateering" was a legal term that meant the people stealing were doing it at the instruction of their governments. Regular pirates worked for themselves. But they did the same thing. It was usually done as a way to steal other countries' wealth. Many countries did this during the 1500s because of the gold and other goods found in the West Indies. One of the reasons the English wanted a colony on the coast of America was to easily reach Spanish ships returning to Spain from the West Indies. The English felt this was the best way to keep Spain from becoming too wealthy and powerful.

North America. England's Queen Elizabeth and her advisor Sir Walter Raleigh also wanted to build colonies in America. If England had colonies, it could stop Spanish ships from returning to Spain with gold and other goods.

England sent two ships to explore America in the spring of 1584. The ships arrived in July at what is today known as the Outer Banks of North Carolina. The English explorers had been in America three days when Native Americans, of the

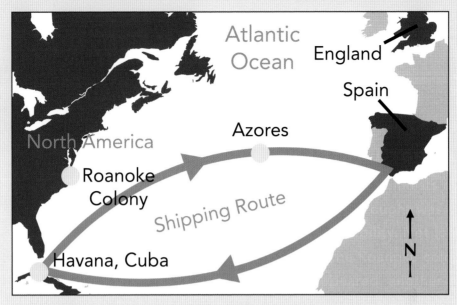

Shipping Treasures from the West Indies

Spain became wealthy from buying and stealing spices and gold in the West Indies. Spanish ships risked being attacked by pirates on the trip back to Spain. The Spanish decided to set up colonies in America to help defend their ships. How do you think the Spanish could protect their ships by having North American colonies? Why would the English try to stop them from having colonies?

Algonquian peoples, came to visit them. The first meetings were friendly. The Englishmen saw there were plenty of animals to hunt and good lands to farm.

The explorers returned to England in August to report what they had seen. After hearing the positive news, Sir Walter Raleigh urged Queen Elizabeth to send more people to America to build a colony. In 1585, 600 men departed England in seven ships. However, as the ships approached land, one of the supply ships ran aground and lost most of the food. Instead of having enough food for 600 people for one year, they only had 20 days of food. Most men returned to England, while 106 of them stayed behind to begin building the fort.

Bad Omens

The English explorers landed 80 miles (130 km) from Roanoke Island, their intended destination. Some of the Englishmen went ashore to meet local Native Americans.

After the Englishmen's arrivals from 1584 to 1585, the Native Americans had seen a total solar eclipse and a comet crossing the sky. They believed these were bad omens. Shortly after the comet—and after numerous visits from the Englishmen—many of the Native Americans began falling sick and dying. They believed this was because of the Englishmen.

Native Americans protected their villages from the English because they did not trust them.

After landing far from their destination, the English continued traveling to Roanoke. They met more Native Americans along the way. The English and Native Americans did not trust each other. The Native Americans worried the English would take too much of their food.

When the English heard a rumor that the Native Americans were going to attack them at Roanoke in the spring of 1586, they killed a Native American chief. The English worried it was dangerous in America. When more English ships arrived in 1586, the group decided to return to England. A hurricane

Men and Women Together

Previous expeditions to Roanoke had carried only men. These men were soldiers, and they were supposed to help battle the Spanish by privateering. The 1587 voyage had men and women who planned to stay in America. People had many reasons for going to America. Some people set sail believing they had better opportunities to own land and farm in America than in England. Some people wanted to escape religious persecution in England. The English knew that in order to build a successful colony they would need families and people with diverse skills.

had destroyed their new ship, and the group did not want to stay any longer.

The English Try Again

Raleigh still wanted to build a colony in America. In 1587 he sent more than 100 people to America to start a colony in Chesapeake Bay. John White, an artist, would be governor of the new colony. White's daughter, Eleanor Dare, was on board the ship and pregnant.

The ship's captain stopped at Roanoke and

refused to go farther. He insisted the colonists build there instead. They began working right away. A few days later, a man named George Howe was attacked and killed by Native Americans when he was alone. To the Europeans, this seemed to be unprovoked. They may not have been aware of the attacks made by the earlier settlers in 1585. White wanted to make peace with one of the Native American tribes and make things safer for his colony. The tribe did not understand what White wanted. In frustration, the colonists attacked the tribe they believed had killed Howe. But they accidentally attacked a friendly tribe, causing more tension and mistrust.

A Change of Plans

On August 18, 1587, Eleanor gave birth to Virginia Dare, the first English person born on American soil. At that point, things looked bad for the colonists. They were not on good terms with local tribes. They were short on supplies. They were not in Chesapeake

The colonists at Roanoke may have gathered together for the baptism of their youngest colony member, Virginia Dare.

Bay where they were supposed to be. It was decided the ships would return to England for more supplies.

White was chosen by the colony to return to England. His plan was to explain the problems to Queen Elizabeth and Raleigh and ask for help. He would return to America as soon as possible with things they needed to survive. The war with Spain prevented White from returning right away. All English ships were needed to fight the Spanish Armada, a fleet of 160 ships. White was worried. How would the colonists survive until his return?

The Roanoke colonists were the first group of English colonists to include both men and women. Historian Karen Ordahl Kupperman explains more about the group of English colonists that set out for America in 1587:

> *A certain amount can be learned from White's own list of the colonists. Judging by coincidence of names, there were fourteen families. Four of the families included a mother, father, and child . . . Two of the women, Margaret Harvie and Eleanor Dare, were so far advanced in pregnancy that their deliveries occurred soon after arrival in Roanoke. Six were married couples without children, and four were fathers and sons who probably expected to be joined by the rest of their families in future voyages.*
>
> Source: Karen Ordahl Kupperman. *Roanoke: The Abandoned Colony.* Totowa, NJ: Rowman & Allanheld, 1984. Print. 6.

Back It Up

Kupperman is using evidence to support a point. Write a paragraph describing this point. Then write two or three pieces of evidence she uses to prove that point.

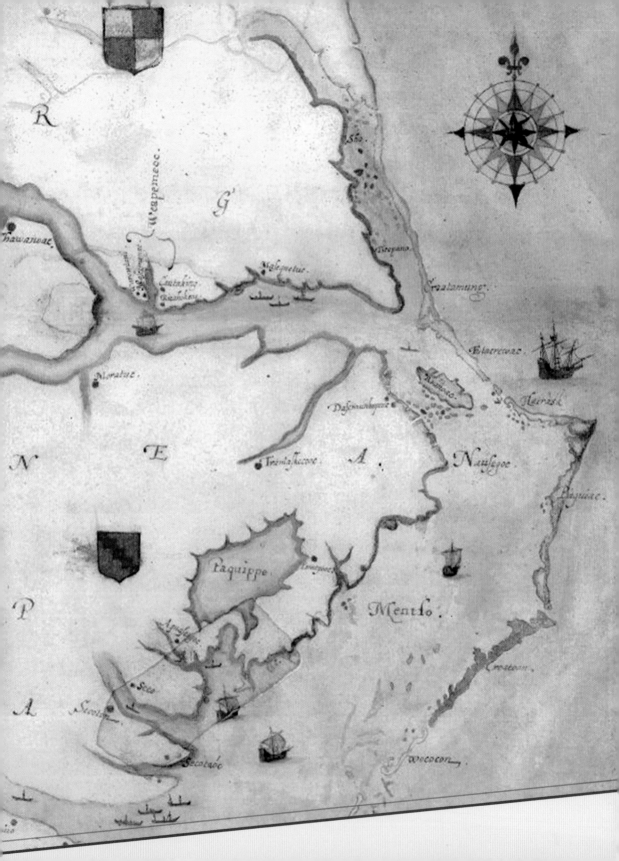

CHAPTER TWO

THE RETURN TO ROANOKE

In the spring of 1588, White finally secured two ships to travel back to America and the colony he left behind. Along the way, however, French ships attacked them. The English were forced to return to England.

White worried about the colonists. Not everyone in England cared as much as he did. It took until 1590 before White boarded a privateering ship headed for

White created this East Coast map in 1585 after his first trip to America.

the West Indies. The ship ran into severe storms as it approached America, making it difficult to land. From the ship, White could see plumes of smoke at Roanoke. He was happy the colonists were still there.

Following the Smoke

The next morning as the ship made it to land, White saw smoke again. The smoke was coming from nearby Haterask Island. He decided to go and look for the colonists. But when he found the source of the smoke, it looked similar to a lightning strike. There were no signs of people or homes.

When White returned to America, he found no signs of his family or of the other colonists he left behind years before.

By the time he returned to the ship, it was almost dark. He had to wait until morning to return to Roanoke. It was August 18, 1590, Virginia Dare's third birthday. There was no one on Roanoke when White arrived. Near where he had left the colonists, White was happy to see a tree with the letters *CRO* carved into it. Before White left in 1587, the colonists talked about trying to move inland. They picked a signal for White. If the colonists moved, they would carve the name of the place where they were going into a tree. If they felt they were in danger, they would also carve a cross over the name. On August 18, there was no cross over the letters on the tree.

White also found another carving on an entrance post that read *CROATOAN*. There was no cross over this word either. Croatoan was the name of a friendly tribe and an island 50 miles (80 km) from Roanoke. The houses at Roanoke had been taken down, not burned. White believed the carvings meant the colonists had moved and had not been in danger.

More Troubles

White's shipmates feared bad weather was coming. After looking for the colonists on Roanoke, they went back to the ship. They planned to leave the next morning for Croatoan. But two of the ships lost their anchors in the storm the night before. The boats were low on food, and the crew had left their drinking water on Roanoke in a hurry to return to the boat.

Instead of traveling to Croatoan, the crew set sail for the West Indies to get more food and water. They would stay there for the winter and sail to Croatoan

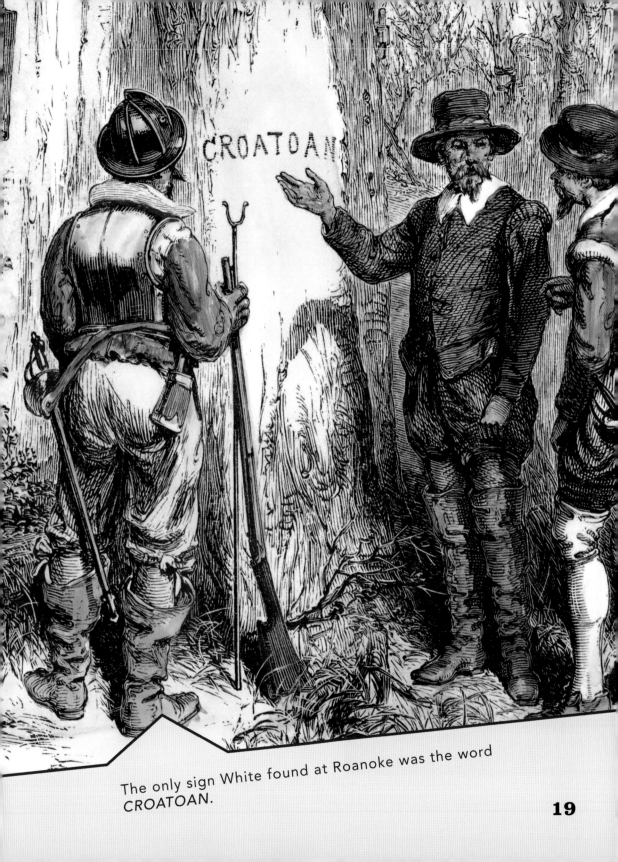

The only sign White found at Roanoke was the word CROATOAN.

in the spring. Before they could do that, another big storm came and swept them out to sea. The ship's captain worried it would be hard to reach the West Indies. Instead he sailed for the Azores, a group of islands in the Atlantic Ocean west of Portugal. After a difficult journey, the ship's crew wanted to return to England to deliver the items they had seized, rather than go back to the West Indies. White could not convince them.

White never returned to America. It was ten more years before another English ship sailed for America. No one could find the colonists when they arrived. Where had the Roanoke colonists gone and why?

Why Didn't White Return to America?

Little is known about White after he returned to England. The war with Spain required all of England's ships to fight the Spanish Armada. There were no ships free to return to America. Then Queen Elizabeth died. After that, the new king put Raleigh into prison for treason. Without the Queen and Raleigh, White had a hard time getting people to help him.

Author David Stick explains why the Roanoke colony may have caused Spain to increase its war efforts against England in 1587:

> *It is ironic that the attempts by Raleigh and his associates to establish a North American colony may have contributed to [Spain's King] Philip's decision to have it out, once and for all, with England. Ever since Columbus established the initial claim in 1492, America had been Spain's private domain, a veritable lode of treasure. . . . Raleigh's colonizing claim to much of the North American continent and Sir Francis Drake's bold and successful raids at the heart of Spain's American colonies were something else again. King Philip reasoned, and rightly so, that England had to be stopped, and soon. How better to cut off the threat than to assemble a flotilla so powerful as to make inevitable the conquering of Elizabeth's naval forces, and even England itself?*
>
> Source: David Stick. Roanoke Island: The Beginnings of English America. *Chapel Hill, NC: University of North Carolina Press, 1983. Print. 156–157.*

What's the Big Idea?

Take a close look at this passage. What is the main connection between Roanoke and the attack on England by the Spanish Armada? What would Spain have to lose if they did not try to stop Roanoke from being settled?

CHAPTER THREE

WHERE DID THE COLONISTS GO?

Since 1590 many people have wondered what happened to the Roanoke colonists. Historians have studied records and stories for years. They have tried to come up with one theory to solve the mystery, but it has not been an easy or successful task. Different theories have been explored throughout the centuries since the colonists' mysterious disappearance. One theory is that Spanish

Raleigh's plan to set up a colony in America failed, but it paved the way for future colonies.

Sir Walter Raleigh

Raleigh was a true believer in building a colony in America. He felt it would make England a stronger country. Queen Elizabeth believed in Raleigh's ideas. She made him a rich and powerful man. But she was not happy when he married one of her ladies-in-waiting. She had both Raleigh and her lady-in-waiting thrown in jail. Later he was freed and worked for the Queen, but she did not like him as much. He no longer had as much power. Without having the Queen on his side, it was hard to get people interested in returning to Roanoke. Some historians wonder what would have happened to Roanoke if Raleigh had not angered the Queen.

soldiers or Native Americans murdered the colonists.

Spanish Privateers Theory

In the late 1500s, war broke out between England and Spain. The Spanish had built colonies in America beginning in 1492. They were useful places to stop when sailing between Spain and the West Indies. They were also a way for the Spanish to gain control in this new land. One of the reasons the English wanted an American

Although the Spanish Armada had hundreds of ships, the English were successful in beating them in 1588.

colony was to use it as a base to attack Spanish ships. When the Spanish found out about the English settling Roanoke, they wanted to stop the colony from succeeding.

However, the Spanish Armada attacked England in 1588. They were not successful. The English beat them badly, and the war continued. If the Spanish had killed the Roanoke colonists, it seems likely the Spanish would have wanted England to know. There is no evidence that any Spaniards ever took credit for killing the Roanoke colonists. There were also no bodies or remains found at Roanoke.

Native American Theory

There were many Native American tribes around Roanoke. Some were friendly, but others were not.

Native American Folklore

Many historians do not believe Native Americans killed the colonists because there is no trace of it in Native American folklore. These stories are important to Native American history. This was how they recorded their beliefs and important events. They told each other the stories to remember their past and their ancestors. Some folktales were known as "hero stories," which described heroic actions by specific Native Americans. If the English had been killed by the Native Americans to protect themselves, they likely would have had a hero story about it. With no folklore that talks about murdering the colonists, it does not seem likely to have taken place.

The English were invading their territory. Others worried there was not enough food to share. Some tribes believed that seeing a comet after the English arrived was a bad omen, meaning the English were evil. When Native Americans began to die of diseases unknown to them, they suspected the English brought the diseases.

The English attacked a tribe in 1587, believing they were hostile. The tribe was not, but after being attacked, they were much less friendly.

There were many reasons the Native Americans feared the English.

No bodies or remains were found at Roanoke colony, or in the area around it. Native Americans are also well known for their oral histories. They pass down stories of their lives from generation to generation. No known Native American history tells of killing off the Roanoke settlers. This would have been important to tribes in the 1500s. If neither the Spanish nor the Native Americans killed the colonists, what happened to them?

FURTHER EVIDENCE

Chapter Three talks about where the colonists could have gone after leaving Roanoke. The article at the website below goes into more depth on this topic. Does the article answer any of the questions you have about the Roanoke colonists?

Roanoke Colonists
mycorelibrary.com/roanoke-colonists

CHAPTER FOUR

DESPERATION OR DROUGHT?

Along with the theories of the Spanish or the Native Americans murdering the Roanoke colonists, there are other ideas. It must have been frightening to be left alone at Roanoke. The colonists hoped White would return in a few months. Eventually they must have realized something was wrong. They did not have much food. They may have

The Roanoke colonists may have attempted the dangerous journey back to England before White returned and found their note.

The local Native Americans may not have had enough food to share with the colonists, forcing the English to try to make the journey overseas.

decided to take a big risk and return to England by taking a small boat that was left behind.

This would have been dangerous, as the boat was not big enough to hold 100 people. Yet when White returned in 1590, the boat was gone. This could mean the colonists tried to cross the Atlantic Ocean. If so, they never arrived in England and it is likely they died at sea.

Though the boat was gone, its absence does not mean the colonists sailed to England. There are many ways the Roanoke colonists' boat could have disappeared. They may have taken the boat with them when they left Roanoke for Croatoan. Or it is possible that other groups such as Native Americans or the Spanish took it.

The Drought

During the time the colonists were at Roanoke, a bad drought struck the Jamestown region and the part of Virginia called the Tidewater, which includes Roanoke Island. Without enough water, it was hard for the colonists to grow

Vegetable/Fruit	Number of Days to Harvest	Latest Date to Plant
Potatoes	95–120	March 15
Sweet corn	85–90	May 15
Watermelon	90–100	June 15
Pumpkin	115–120	July 1
Lima beans	65–80	July 15
Cucumbers	56–65	August 1
Winter squash	70–95	August 1
Carrots	75–80	September 1
Snap beans	50–55	September 15

Not Enough Time to Grow Food

The Roanoke colonists did not arrive until August 1587. In order to grow enough food to last them over the winter, they would have had to start planting in May. Many crops take two or three months to grow. August would have been too late to start. How do you think this growing season would have affected the colonists' food supply? Do you think other food was available for them to eat?

food. Animals would have had a hard time finding enough to eat and drink.

The colonists did not have time to plant their own garden when they first arrived in 1587. They would have relied on what they could find in the forest and what animals they could hunt or fish. The Native Americans would also have been short of food. It would have been hard for them to share what they had if it was not enough for their own village. It is possible the drought made it too hard for them to survive, and they starved to death.

However, there were no graves or bodies found at the colony. If the colonists were starving, they would have been too weak to go elsewhere. Later searchers would have found traces of the colonists' bodies if they had starved to death on their journey to Croatoan. Since no bodies have been found at or near Roanoke, is it possible the colonists moved and lived elsewhere? Some historians believe so.

Learning about Droughts

Scientists who are interested in the lost colony of Roanoke discovered the drought in the trees. Bald cypress trees can grow for hundreds of years. Just as scientists can tell the age of a tree from the rings inside it, scientists can look at the rings in bald cypress trees to find evidence of drought and wildfires. Trees in the Roanoke area show strong signs of drought during the time the colonists were there.

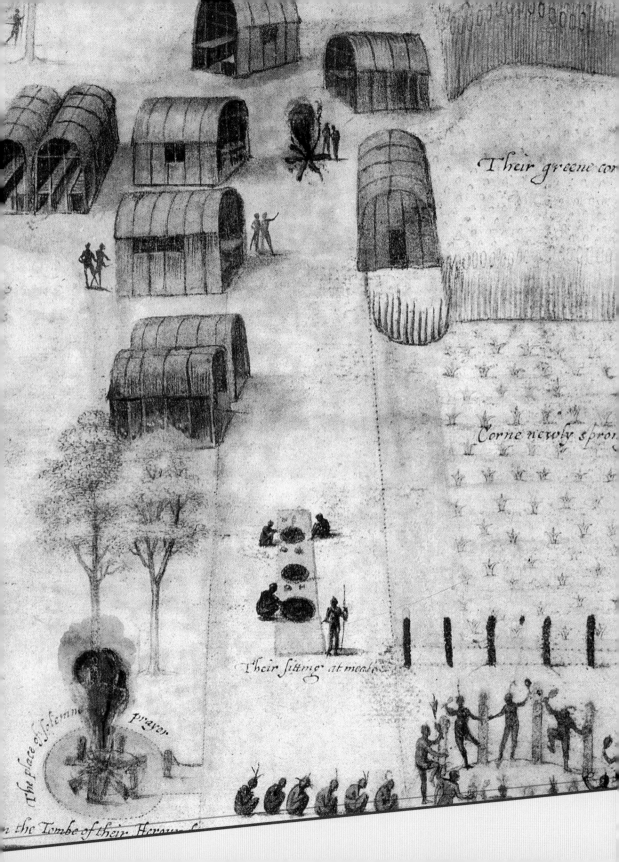

Their greene cor[n]

Corne newly spro[ng]

Their sitting at meate

The place of solemne prayer

o[n] the Tombe of their Heroun [...]

DID THE COLONISTS SURVIVE?

Many theories suggest the colonists died. The colonists may have tried to leave Roanoke for Croatoan but did not make it. They may have met Native Americans who allowed them to join their tribe and spend the rest of their lives with them.

The colonists should have known that White would not return for several months because of the

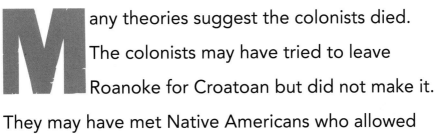

It is possible the missing colonists joined local Native American tribes after White did not return to the colony.

Eleanor Dare's "Diary"

In the 1930s, large stones with English words carved into them were found in Georgia. They had the initials E. W. D. Could the letters stand for Eleanor White Dare? People were excited at the thought of Eleanor joining a tribe and moving to Georgia. The stones told the story of Eleanor's father and daughter being killed by Native Americans. However, in 1941 a journalist wrote an article about the stones. He brought in experts who knew that some of the words on the stones were modern. It also appeared the carving in the stones was not old enough. The stones were a hoax.

time it took to cross the Atlantic Ocean. They also would have realized they did not have enough food and resources to survive the winter at Roanoke.

The colonists had already made a plan to let White know where they had gone if they left—by carving the name of their destination where he could see it. White found a carving that read *CROATOAN*. There was no sign the colonists felt they were in danger. Yet, later settlers at Croatoan

A stone with the words "Virgin Dare Died Here, Captif Powhatan, 1590, Charles R" was found in North Carolina in 1924. It was fake.

found no evidence the Roanoke colonists arrived there.

However, there are stories among both later settlers and Native Americans about English people living with local tribes. The Lumbee tribe later claimed the Roanoke colonists were their ancestors. There were also stories about tribe members with gray or blue eyes and blond hair. Reverend Morgan Jones reported in 1660 that he talked to Native Americans with light skin who could speak Welsh.

In 1709 John Lawson published a book about the Carolinas that said Native Americans around Roanoke reported having white ancestors. Native Americans normally do not have gray or blue eyes or blond hair. If the Roanoke colonists had children with Native Americans, that could happen.

Some tribes near Roanoke also reported having members who could read and write English at a time when most Native Americans could not. These tribes also recalled seeing Native Americans wearing clothes similar to those of the English. Several tribes around Roanoke have claimed they have white ancestors, and that these ancestors were the Roanoke colonists.

Is It True?

It is hard to know if this theory of the Roanoke colonists joining a Native American tribe is correct. Native Americans often relate their history through folktales. Many of these tales talk about tribe members that could have been the lost colonists. There were more than 100 colonists left at Roanoke

More fake stones were found in 1939.

when White returned to England. That would have been more people than any one tribe could support, so it would have made sense for the colonists to separate.

Relics in Croatoan

Archaeologists have found relics, such as an ax head, a coin, and a signet ring, that date back to the 1600s in the area around Croatoan, now called Hatteras Island. The items appear to be European, not Native American. There is also work being done with radar to uncover relics and even buildings that have been buried for hundreds of years. Although there is little evidence showing the colonists arrived in Croatoan, it is possible Native Americans traded these items to other settlers in the area. That would add to the theory that the colonists joined Native American tribes.

It is also possible that as the colonists traveled to Croatoan, they met Native Americans who had been attacked by the English. The colonists may have been taken as prisoners or slaves. If the tribes roamed in search of food, the colonists would have left the area around Roanoke and traveled with the tribes.

After hundreds of years of research, no historian knows the correct answer to what happened to the Roanoke colonists. The fact that they left Roanoke and did not appear to be in distress seems to suggest that they left of their own free will and traveled to Croatoan. What happened after they left Roanoke is the mystery. With the little evidence historians have gathered, the most they can do is imagine what might have happened to the Roanoke colonists.

EXPLORE ONLINE

Chapter Five discusses whether or not the colonists left Roanoke and lived with Native American tribes. What is the main point of this chapter? What key evidence supports this point? The website at the link below discusses relics found at Cape Hatteras. Find a quote on this website that supports the main point of this chapter.

Relics Found in Cape Hatteras

mycorelibrary.com/roanoke-colonists

The colonists were killed.

Evidence for:

• Both the Spanish and the Native Americans had motives.

Evidence against:

• No bodies were found. There is nothing in Native American history that discusses Roanoke.

A severe drought occurred and the colonists died from starvation.

Evidence for:

• The colony appeared to have been taken apart as if the colonists were moving elsewhere.

Evidence against:

• No bodies were found.

The colonists took a small boat back to England. They were lost at sea.

Evidence for:

• The boat John White left behind was missing.

Evidence against:

- The colonists left signs that they were going to Croatoan.

The colonists joined Native American tribes.

Evidence for:

- There are tales about tribe members who could read and write.

Evidence against:

- Folklore can sometimes be fiction.

STOP AND THINK

Tell the Tale

Chapter Two discusses John White's return to Roanoke. Imagine you are White, finding the empty colony and the word *CROATOAN* carved on a post and *CRO* carved on a tree. Write 200 words about what you think happened to the colonists and what you would do to find them.

Surprise Me

This book discusses theories of what happened to the Roanoke colonists. After reading this book, what two or three facts did you find most surprising? Write a few sentences about each fact. Why did you find each fact surprising?

Dig Deeper

After reading this book, what questions do you still have about the lost colony of Roanoke? With an adult's help, find a few reliable sources that can help you answer your questions. Write a paragraph about what you learned.

Say What?

Learning about history in America and Europe can mean learning a lot of new vocabulary. Find five words in this book you've never heard before. Use a dictionary to find out what they mean. Then write the meanings in your own words, and use each word in a sentence.

GLOSSARY

archaeologists
scientists that study bones and tools of ancient people to learn about their lives and activities

armada
a large number of warships working together

drought
a period of time in which there is little or no rain

folklore
stories that a culture passes down from one generation to the next

hoax
to trick someone

ladies-in-waiting
women who serve as help to a queen or princess

omens
things that serve as signs or warnings for the future

oral histories
stories about family and community that are passed down from generation to generation

privateers
men who have been authorized by their government to attack and steal valuables from other ships

theory
an idea that might explain facts or events

LEARN MORE

Books

Horn, James. *A Kingdom Strange: The Brief and Tragic History of the Lost Colony of Roanoke.* New York: Basic, 2010.

Kupperman, Karen Ordahl. *Roanoke: The Abandoned Colony.* Lanham, MD: Rowman & Littlefield, 2007.

McAneney, Caitie. *The Lost Colony of Roanoke.* New York: PowerKids Press, 2015.

Websites

To learn more about Mysteries of History, visit **booklinks.abdopublishing.com.** These links are routinely monitored and updated to provide the most current information available.

Visit **mycorelibrary.com** for free additional tools for teachers and students.

INDEX

ABOUT THE AUTHOR

Amy C. Rea is a writer from Minnesota. She loves to read, write, and hang out with her kids and dog. She has always been fascinated by stories about settlers and mysteries.